Emotionally
Constipated

Purging Through Poetry

J. C. Sands

Jo Sands Voice Productions
Monroe, GA
Printed in the USA

Requests for permission should be addressed in writing to:
Jo Sands Voice Productions
1430 Waterford Lane
Monroe, GA 30656.

Emotionally Constipated/J.C. Sands
1. Non-Fiction-Poetry
2. Non-Fiction-General

Paperback ISBN-13: 979-8-9852726-1-1
eBook ISBN-13: 979-8-9852726-0-4
Audiobook ISBN-13: 979-8-9852726-2-8

Library of Congress Control Number: 2022905800

Cataloging-in-Publication Data is on file with the Library of Congress.

Printed in the United States of America
10 9 8 7 6 5 4 3 2 1

What Others Are Saying About This Book

"It isn't often that I stop to pick up a book of poetry to read. However, when I was given a copy of "Emotionally Constipated" to review, the title intrigued me enough to open it up and take a look. I could relate to every poem in the book. The author's lyrics are clear, clean, and revealing of her journey from hopeful to heartbroken, to angry and bitter, to finding that moment where the realization comes that what is toxic isn't what is in other people, but what is in you, and writing is the only way to get all of that crap out of your system. I highly recommend picking up a copy for anyone who just might find themselves a little emotionally constipated after going through trauma."

– Brandy M. Miller, International speaker, Award-Winning Author & CEO of 40 Day Writer LLC

"Reading "Emotionally Constipated" was a literary laxative to the soul. Jo's honesty pours onto the pages in a poetic voice like a diuretic. This is a read for anyone that had a moment they could not get over, to purge it from themselves through reading the book. It is an example of excellence in the art of poetry with a purpose."

- Jade & Wilnona, the "And We Thought Ladies," Award-winning Poets, www.andwethought.com

Contents

When love calls...or was it a misdial?

Teenage Love

He was my middle school crush
back in the day,
Talent show rapper
with faded waves.
A handsome smile
had all the girls blushing
Walking down the hallways,
Had all the girls wishing
For a wink, a hug,
Or a moment of time
But he was so mannish,
Grabbing girl's behinds.

My computer love
At the high school dance,
I watched him across the gym,
I didn't stand a chance.
Like Bruce Leroy,
I didn't have any moves,
So I swayed on the wall

Emotionally Constipated

To every tune of the grooves.

The end of the year
he finally spoke to me
It was like slow motion,
Him approaching me.
Green Apple Now-N-Later
Nearly choking me,
And when he smiled,
It nearly blinded me.

I waited for him to say
How much he was liking me,
But all I heard was
"Why are your teeth so green?"
I wanted to die as he walked away
Green Apple Now-N-Later
Had him fading away...

Now we're all grown up,
And finally reconnected.
22 years later
and I happily accepted
His friend request
As he was checking me out,
Seeing how all these years
Had filled me out.

No more green smiles,
This girl was full grown,
Grown into the best woman
He had ever known.
The talent show boy
Had grown into a real man.

My heart skipped a beat
When he took my hand.

Soul sipping,
He had my mind tripping,
Body trembling…
He had my hips dipping.
Legs shaking…
My oven started baking,
Had me screaming
Betty Crocker
…I want to rock with ya!

My best friend,
My one and only man.
Smooth dark chocolate
With the velvet hands.
My ever after would be
Forever after
In love with him,
The past didn't matter

We argued, debated,
For love we elevated.
Until we graduated,
And a ceremony dated
To seal what God created.
So pure and genuine,
I had his heart
And he had mine,
A true love
Of a lifetime.

The Beginning

Warm rays softly caress tender cheeks
as tendrils of ebony curls
sway gently in the breeze.

Emblazoned orbs of liquid fire
slowly melt the sheerest of
chiffons

Time stands still when

two hearts
collide.

Sounds become
words in a language
only they understand.

With a conjugal promise of forever
entwined with intimate petals of love.

Why or What?

Here I sit
Thinking of you.
I don't know
Why or what
To do.

My heart pounds
As love soars.
I'm floating on air
Sailing out the door.

Away from my desk
Escaping these numbers,
To reminisce about a love
That never slumbers.

I love being
In love with you.
It leaves me not
Knowing why

Emotionally Constipated

Or what to do.

Letter To My Love

Another day of work and stress,
I can hardly wait to get home and undress.

To take off all the corporate phoniness,
The mundane rules and foolishness.
Forgetting all the lies relayed
Of Friday's coming and getting paid.

Although, to some
this meant getting laid,
or whatever object
for life they trade,
yet that style is not for me.

Oh no. I am someone's special lady.
And after I send my prayers above,
I quietly sit and write a letter
To my love.

When things go from Sugar to S*$!

Ordinary Life of a Tired Wife

Too tired to cry
Too tired to lie.
Neck needs cracking,
Body justa aching.
Here the boss goes again
Trying to call me back in.

This fan is blowing hot air
I need to put on new underwear.
It's hotter than hot can be in this house
With two small rooms
And one lumpy couch.

Hey!
Who drank all the sweet tea?
I've been working all day
And none is left for me?

House is a mess
And cooking for two,

Emotionally Constipated

It's never ending,
Always something to do.

Ouch!
My big toe!
He has one more time
To leave his junk in the floor.

Taking me for granted,
Real soon I'm gonna leave,
After I rest on this lumpy couch
And make some sweet tea.

Counseling Session

Date nights?
We do not date anymore,
That shipped sailed
A long time ago,
And its parked outside
Another woman's door.

He thinks I don't know
When he's on the late-night creep.
Unfortunately, he just can't
Stay out of other people's sheets.

Excuse me?
I am traditional,
Never boring.
Besides, she can have him
With all his obnoxious snoring.

I did the best I could
Worked, cooked, and cleaned.

Emotionally Constipated

If that wasn't enough
Then its best we both leave.

I came here so you could fix him,
Thanks, but no thanks for your time.
These sessions are on you, Doc,
I'm not giving you a dime.

Rage

The rage swells
Like a storm across the sea
Churning the murky waters
Engulfing me.
Sails of surrender billows
As the wind blows,
Ignored by the wrath
Which continues to grow.
Anchors swim
As the ship tosses and turns,
Hearts blister
From angry word burns.
Tears like rain
Wash cheeks of pain.
Storm clouds brewing
In eyes subduing.
Hopeless drifting,
The storm is shifting.
Lightning flashes
As waves crash

Emotionally Constipated

Into stubborn rocks.
I cannot see
No lighthouse lantern guiding me.
The Krakens unleashed
A battle of wills at hand,
No haven
For woman or man,
Until the storm subsides
And rests the ship on dry land.

The End

Numbness creeps in
As darkness waits
The stench of a rotting relationship
Permeates through the air.

Foul belches of loneliness
Erupt from porcelain hearts
Stained with the residue
Of expired love.

Cryptic silhouettes
Roam aimlessly about
Twin mouths too hollow to shout.

Liquid pools dammed in tired eyes
Reflect the cruel judgement
Of Father Time.

A masculine shadow nods slowly
As the feminine fragrance

Emotionally Constipated

Of bitter ire wafts past.

The scent of home.

Life happens at the
most unexpected times

Pandemic Prayer

Lord,
I'm choking
Can't breathe
So much grief and sorrow
Surrounding me.
Every day another death
Undertaker gets a dollar,
The pills of pain
Are too big to swallow.
The war with principalities
Is trying to get the best of
me.
Like Job, I stay on bended
knee,
Holding on
Staying strong.

Tonight, I weep tears with weary eyes,
And pray to celebrate your love and mercy
In the morning should I rise.

Farewell

What a joyful day to see you take your
first breath,
A mother's love is unbounded and will
never ever rest.
Watching your first steps,
even your first day of school,
Brings back warm memories of how you
made your own rules.
Watching you grow into womanhood to see the
lives you touched,
Has been such a blessing and means so
much.
Finally, watching as you take your last
breath,
Although, it was hard for me to do,
God whispered, "It's ok because I love her
too."

One Nation Under a WTF?

Brick by brick
Stone by stone
United we stand
Yet, walk alone.

Burping bile of bigotry
Raising legacies of idolatry
No rest for the weary
Or faint of heart
United we stand
Divided we part.

Melting pot of messiness
Crayons stuffed in boxes
broken, shattered pieces
heartless souls unleashing
Bitterness, rage, and greed
What more could we possibly need?

Let Whose Freedom Ring?

Who decides on this deceptive ride,
When is it decided who is wrong or right?
To dance in white sheets
And ride at midnight?

What strange fruits we harvest
From the bitter trees
The burden of bigotry
bowing bent knees

When will we all be free?
When is freedom due to me?
Will it ever be?

Knees in necks,
Out of breath
We take for granted
Senseless deaths.

How can we be free?

Emotionally Constipated

Do you even see me?
When you look, what do you see?
A threat to society?
Can you not love me for me?

A nation built on the backs of millions
Rotting in graves,
Fertilizing the land of the free
Home of the brave.
Through the dreams of doctors,
Servicemen, lawyers, the hope
Of the slave.

Retribution's Song

Take a pill for the pain
Swallow up the stain
Digest the enormity
Conformity
Hypocrisy
Fallacy of being
Just another
Strong black woman.

Strong enough to
Bare the penetration
Of verbal dagger's concentration
On points of weakness
Descending through fleshless
Folds of meekness
Piercing ages of pride,
A heritage birthed
With each stride.

Black enough to deflect the shame

Emotionally Constipated

Woman enough to kiss the rain
Of bitterness
Clinging like hope
From a cherry spout.

So sure of its gain
A matchless victory
The pride of contempt
Fails to see the whimsicality,

A cranial tilt
Eyes illuminated with a galaxy of stars
Blinding truth-shielding fields of scars.

Intoxicated with sweet venom nectar
The seduction of ageless anger and disdain,
Its putrid aroma of prejudice reigns
As only a distant memory.

Blades dulled by matchless grace
Contorted faces of distorted rhetoric
Painted with daisies of retribution,
Bones of bitterness
Brittle in confusion,
Autographed by a sway
Of rapaciousness.

A nation of pride swells
Impenetrable sails
As carnage descends
Into murky depths,
Victory eclipsed
Foremothers wept.

And just like that...
another one shows up

Dreaming of Another Man

Let me tickle your fancy
And take a sip of your soul,
Meditate on your mental
And lick your lips till I'm full.

Let me cradle your cranium,
Give your marrow a rest,
Swaddled in luscious mounds
As high as Mt. Everest.

And as we lay down
So gently to sleep,
I pray that my heart
You will securely keep.

Embraced in this reality
Of the realization of this gravity,
Weighing heavy on my mind
Because we are running out of time.

Emotionally Constipated

Or is this the beginning
of a beautiful happy ending?
It's like the world's against us
and everybody else is winning.

So, for now I sit still
with paper and quill
Rewriting this love story
in my mind,
Erasing and tracing
looking for an end I can deal with.
Alarm goes off
I guess we ran out of time.

Him

He challenged me to
Wrestle against old chains
Binding the doors of my imagination,
Once upon a time my only protection.

Provoked to strive further
Higher than ever before.
Stretching my mind,
Leaving me wanting more.

Implored me
To stay true to me
Because he adores all of me.

To touch him, smell him
My senses are open
Receptive, ready, willing to accept
All the wonderful flavors.
Ready to savor
The essence of him.

Emotionally Constipated

Open and free,
Ready to share the best with me.
He saved no less for me
As though he knew that I could accept
No less than what he could
Never give the rest.
Keys unlocking doors and chests,
Protecting a healed heart
Laying in rest.
Awaiting to be ignited, excited,
Ready to be invited
To receive the best of him.

The Confession

Lord,
I loved a man who was not you,
He never did the things you could do,
But I clung to him and would not let go
My life tossed and turned,
Was this friend or foe?
I did not wait as you
had asked,
Strayed on a course
of rocky paths.
Then one day
after feeling all
alone,
I remembered
you were sitting
upon a throne.
On bended knees,
Through tears of shame
I prayed to you and cried out your name.
To the water you had me go

Emotionally Constipated

to drown a mountain
of fears and woes.
You washed my face
And dried the tears

Then said, "For you,
I have waited years.
Here is the path,
I have paved the way.
Just follow me,
No need to stray.
The journey is long,
I have packed your bags,
Your name is engraved,
No need for tags.
We won't take a plane,
train, or bike.
On this journey we will
have to hike.
I want to be alone with you,
Without any distractions,
To give you the attention you need
And restore your laughter.
To show you how the daughter of the king will live
So, when court jesters come to perform,
Attention you will not give.
Oh, and the smooth crooner with dashing charms,
Are no match for these loving arms.
With me, you are never alone,
I came to help show you the way home.
My love will never keep you out in the cold,
I will take care of your needs
even when you grow old."
But, Lord, I have to carry my own bags?

"The weight you carry are pounds of bless-   ings,
Included with my words, and a few   les-
sons.
When the days get long,
And the path grows dreary,
Lean on them should
you get weary.
And never you mind,
I am just a little further up the
way,
Clearing the path for you day by
day.
Walk in the light, do not fear,
Our Father is waiting,
Your voice he will always hear."

The sun always shines after rain and hurricanes

An Excerpt from Dirty Seeds

Mootsies was packed with the usual Friday night regulars. Smooth jazz wafted throughout the brownstone building all the way down Broad Street. White linens covered thirty small round tables throughout the dining room, all balancing duplicate ornate crystal lanterns in their centers.

A grand stage with heavy midnight curtains to the left of the entranceway was being set up with equipment for the night's performance.

Monica had recovered from her afternoon ordeal and was seated in their favorite corner table to the right of the stage with Janelle, Sharon, and Naomi. They had been through a lot together, but even with their hectic schedules still managed to get together once a month for some much needed "girl time."

"So, who was this handsome stranger you met today, Mo?" Naomi asked while sipping her sparkling water through a tiny red straw. Her flawless chestnut skin glowed in the dim light of the room. Long, curly ringlets escaped an updo piled high on top of her head and cascaded around her heart shaped face. Naomi was a huntress.

Monica turned an accusing stare towards Sharon. "Sharon, you can't hold water," Monica chided.

"I know that's right," Janelle chimed in. "The last time I told Sharon anything I ended up divorced with a stack of bills sky high!" Her large gold hoops cast small rainbows in her twisted locs falling neatly around her shoulders.

Janelle was the epitome of an African queen. Her strong features were regal and elegant. Her tall, thin frame draped in a multi-colored sheath baring one shoulder.

"You should be thanking me," Sharon protested, "You know Rodney was no good for you."

"Or anybody else for that matter," Naomi finished.

Laughter erupted around the table. Rodney had indeed been a proverbial leech. A businessman with no apparent business. He continuously found one grand opportunity after another that was sure to make him a millionaire one day. All he needed was a willing investor. After a six-month whirlwind romance, he somehow convinced Janelle to marry him.

There were always different reasons why he had to move in with her instead of them both living at his up-state high rise, which had been under renovations for over a year.

Two years into the marriage and thousands of dollars later,

Janelle discovered him for the fraud he was and filed for divorce.

Sharon dabbed her eyes with the corner of a napkin clutched tightly in her hand. "The truth shall set you free!" she exclaimed, holding her right palm in the air.

Although the daughter of an extremely strict minister, Sharon was the most outspoken, humorous one in the group. Her peach skin flushed with laughter as she embarked upon an impromptu sermon of Rodney's.

"That man, I said, that man, ah was a no-good man-ah. He had no business, ah, doing any business, ah, with anybody, ah, because he was a no-body, ah, with no car, ah, and no job, ah, and no house, ah, to lay his head, ah. So, we say farewell, ah, to Brother Rodney, hah, and we say thank you, hah, for giving us eyes to see, weeelllll, and ears to hear, hah, and feet to run, run, run, from a no business, nobody, trying to steal everybody's joy! AAAAMEENNN"

"Hallelujah!" The ladies giggled in unison.

Monica surmised Sharon would have made a dynamic preacher. She looked across the table at Janelle and noticed the tears of joy glittering in her eyes. It was so good seeing the dark days behind her dear friend. The fact that she could now laugh at her past with Rodney was proof her heart had moved on to a better place.

Never bitter, Janelle took time for healing herself and her finances. Her salon had been doing record numbers over the past year.

Emotionally Constipated

"Uh hmm, Mo, you still have not answered my question. Who was this guy you met?" Naomi pressed.

"Why do you want to know so badly?" Janelle defended. Of course, they all knew why. Naomi was a self-proclaimed single woman for life who enjoyed collecting male interests. She was smart, independent, and owned her own boutique of antiques.

"Down, girl!" Sharon laughed. "Get behind me, Satan."

Monica let out a long sigh. Naomi was not going to let this subject go anytime soon, which is exactly why Monica did not call her before dinner like she did with Janelle. Janelle happened to have been on the phone with Sharon, thus the three-way call. Monica took a long drink of her tropical concoction adorned with tidbits of colorful fruit before speaking.

"He was no one in particular. I only know his name, Michael Anderson. He helped me when I became over heated at the track today. That is it. End of story," Monica hurriedly explained. She did not want to think about the incident or him anymore.

"Uhm hmm," Naomi snorted. "Sharon said he only had on a pair of shorts and nothing else..." Naomi reached into her studded purse and pulled out a stick of chewing gum. She slowly unwrapped it and placed it on her tongue. Deliberately chewing while keeping her eyes on Monica for more juicy morsels.

"Girl, please! Can we just enjoy one night without you going on the prowl?" Janelle admonished.

"I declare, you have a serious problem," Sharon added.

Naomi scowled at Janelle and poked her tongue out at Sharon.

"I was just wondering why I have not been lucky enough to meet him yet. This is a small town, you know. If there was someone new here, I would have heard about him already. Besides, I am on the town council's welcoming committee. I have to be hospitable," Naomi cooed.

Monica rolled her eyes. "Well, it looks like your luck is about to change," she groaned.

Envy

If you could see the world
through my eyes,
what would you see?

With so much supposed love
dwells as much evil and envy.

Couples pledging vows for life,
husband counting down the minutes
to cheat on his wife.

Friends huddle close
            pinky swearing
Deacon noticing that new dress
            you are wearing.

One, two, three, red, right!
the dangerous games
we are made to play in the night.

Emotionally Constipated

A baby's squeal is the sound of joy,
it is the silent screams
      we choose to
ignore.

Red, yellow, black, and
white,
are we not still pre-
cious in his sight?

There is no sun when
the darkness falls
no laughter, no love,
no sound at all.

Down this road
you dare not travel,
demons prey upon the
weak
      the soul unravels.

Walk away and never look back,
for into the eyes you envied
      there is no turning back.

The Laxative

Writing is a laxative
That soothes emotional constipation,
Breaking down walls
Of decayed rage, stress, and agitation.
Flushing out decades of fears and uncried tears.
Cleansing the raw flesh of self-rebirth
Swaddling the soul.
Words shielded with layers of invincibility,
For within one can be whomever
They choose to be.
Go wherever imagination takes flight,
Morning, noon, or the darkest of nights.

Writing is a fickle, loyal love.
Its mood changes constantly
Albeit, forever true.
Sword of champions
Defender of the meek.
For in words, the courageousness
Of the weakling speaks.

Emotionally Constipated

The aged bridge over troubled waters
Guiding to the lushness of green valleys
Where eagles soar over mountain tops
To wallow in clouds,
A beacon of light that shines
As storm clouds gather on the horizon.

Words are the fountain of youth
Withstanding the test of time.
Tradition of generations,
The evidence of things not seen.
Wands of hope, for within
Love is spread with the power of a pen.

Writing enhances by elevating the mind
And allows it to remain unchained.
It is a freedom fought hard for,
An inheritance from the enslaved,
A legacy given by those who silently whisper on the winds
and shout with claps of thunder.

Telling untold stories to itchy ears,
Revealing unforgotten secrets.

Writing has saved many a mere mortal
from the depths of wrath,
Quelling the thirst for lethal verbal assaults.
A place of peace that quiets the world,
And allows my mind to speak.

About the Author

J.C. Sands grew up in rural North Florida where she culti-
vated a passion for writing. She is an author, freelance jour-
nalist, entrepreneur, public speaker, podcaster, and serves
on several non-profit boards.

As founder and president of the non-profit organization,
"The Jo Sands Voice Write Don't Fight Project," she seeks
to implement creative writing initiatives for victims of trau-
ma, domestic violence, and at-risk youth and produce their
stories to help with the healing process.

The "Jo Show Podcast" is her voyage into the lives of cre-
atives from all around the globe.

She now calls Georgia her new adoptive home where she
lives with her son, Jimmie, and shih-tzu, Bella.

Please visit her website: www.josandsvoice.com